PERSONNEL RECOVERY OPERATIONS

Air Force Doctrine Document 3-50
1 June 2005

Interim Change 2 (Last Review), 1 November 2011

This document complements related discussion found in Joint Publication 3-50 series.

BY ORDER OF THE
SECRETARY OF THE AIR FORCE

AIR FORCE DOCTRINE DOCUMENT 3-50
1 JUNE 2005
INCORPORATING INTERIM CHANGE 2, 1 NOVEMBER 2011

SUMMARY OF CHANGES

The Air Force Doctrine Working Group has reviewed this document and recommended that it remains valid and will again be reviewed no later than April 2013. This Interim change to Air Force Doctrine Document (AFDD) 2-1.6 changes the cover to AFDD 3-50, *Personnel Recovery Operations* to reflect revised AFI 10-1301, Air Force Doctrine (9 August 2010). AFDD numbering has changed to correspond with the joint doctrine publication numbering architecture. AFDD titles and content remain unchanged until updated in the next full revision. A margin bar indicates newly revised material.

Old Number	New Number	Title
AFDD 2-1	changed to AFDD 3-1	*Air Warfare*
AFDD 2-1.1	changed to AFDD 3-01	Counterair Operations
AFDD 2-1.2	changed to AFDD 3-70	Strategic Attack
AFDD 2-1.3	changed to AFDD 3-03	Counterland Operations
AFDD 2-1.4	changed to AFDD 3-04	Countersea Operations
AFDD 2-1.6	changed to AFDD 3-50	Personnel Recovery Operations
AFDD 2-1.7	changed to AFDD 3-52	Airspace Control
AFDD 2-1.8	changed to AFDD 3-40	Counter-CBRN
AFDD 2-1.9	changed to AFDD 3-60	Targeting
AFDD 2-10	changed to AFDD 3-27	Homeland Operations
AFDD 2-12	changed to AFDD 3-72	Nuclear Operations
AFDD 2-2	changed to AFDD 3-14	Space Operations
AFDD 2-2.1	changed to AFDD 3-14.1	Counterspace Operations
AFDD 2-3	changed to AFDD 3-24	Irregular Warfare
AFDD 2-3.1	changed to AFDD 3-22	Foreign Internal Defense
AFDD 2-4	changed to AFDD 4-0	Combat Support
AFDD 2-4.1	changed to AFDD 3-10	Force Protection
AFDD 2-4.2	changed to AFDD 4-02	Health Services
AFDD 2-4.4	changed to AFDD 4-11	Bases, Infrastructure… [Rescinded]
AFDD 2-4.5	changed to AFDD 1-04	Legal Support
AFDD 2-5	changed to AFDD 3-13	Information Operations
AFDD 2-5.1	changed to AFDD 3-13.1	Electronic Warfare
AFDD 2-5.3	changed to AFDD 3-61	Public Affairs Operations
AFDD 2-6	changed to AFDD 3-17	Air Mobility Operations
AFDD 2-7	changed to AFDD 3-05	Special Operations
AFDD 2-8	changed to AFDD 6-0	Command and Control
AFDD 2-9	changed to AFDD 2-0	ISR Operations
AFDD 2-9.1	changed to AFDD 3-59	Weather Operations

Supersedes: AFDD 2-1.6, 15 July 2000
OPR: LeMay Center/DD
Certified by: LeMay Center/DD
Pages: 41
Accessibility: Available on the e-publishing website at www.e-publishing.af.mil for downloading
Releasability: There are no releasability restrictions on this publication
Approved by: LeMay Center/CC, Maj Gen Thomas K. Andersen, USAF
Commander, LeMay Center for Doctrine Development and Education

FOREWORD

Throughout their history, America's armed forces have maintained a commitment to recover any isolated personnel from hostile or uncertain environments, and denied areas. But until recently, each Service tackled the personnel recovery conundrum unilaterally. For example, the last edition of this document focused on combat search and rescue—the Air Force's mechanism for the recovery of Airmen.

Experiences during Operations ENDURING FREEDOM and IRAQI FREEDOM, as well as lessons learned and relearned since the demise of the Soviet Union suggest that each Service must do a better job of integrating doctrine, tactics, techniques, and procedures. In order to clarify each Service's responsibilities, with regard to personnel recovery, the Chairman of the Joint Chiefs of Staff established a new directive in July 2004.

With Joint Publication 3-50, *Joint Doctrine for Personnel Recovery*, still in draft form, the Chairman of the Joint Chiefs of Staff Instruction 3270.01A outlines the Department of Defense's personnel recovery concept and serves as a starting point for this document. Based on this and other guidance, each Service has had to reconsider the doctrine that outlines how each organizes, trains, and equips forces capable of providing an integrated joint capability to Combatant Commanders.

Air Force Doctrine Document (AFDD) 2-1.6, *Personnel Recovery Operations*, establishes the Air Force's perspective on the joint PR construct. It shifts focus from the rescue of aircrews to the recovery of any isolated personnel. Although the Air Force has always been committed to the recovery of any isolated personnel, previous AFDDs have overly focused on the rescue of aircrews. While the Air Force will continue to maintain its natural emphasis on the recovery of Airmen, this AFDD refines our doctrinal sight picture and affirms that Air Force personnel recovery forces remain committed to the recovery of any isolated personnel.

BENTLEY B. RAYBURN
Major General, USAF
Commander, Headquarters
Air Force Doctrine Center

TABLE OF CONTENTS

INTRODUCTION

> *Those who are possessed of a definitive body of doctrine and of deeply rooted convictions upon it will be in a much better position to deal with the shifts and surprises of daily affairs than those who are merely taking short views...*
>
> **—Winston Churchill**

PURPOSE

Air Force Doctrine Document (AFDD) 2-1.6, *Personnel Recovery Operations (PRO)*, contains the operational-level Air Force views on the Department of Defense's personnel recovery (PR) system. It expounds on AFDD 1, *Air Force Basic Doctrine,* and basic air warfare doctrine contained in AFDD 2-1, *Air Warfare*. Additionally, it establishes the Air Force's viewpoint of the joint PR system. It supersedes AFDD 2-1.6, dated 15 July 2000.

APPLICATION

This AFDD applies to all Airmen. Collectively, the term Airman refers to all active duty, Air Force Reserve, Air National Guard, and civilian Air Force personnel.

The doctrine in this document is authoritative, but not directive. Therefore, commanders need to consider the contents of this AFDD and the particular situation when accomplishing their missions. Airmen should read it, discuss it, and practice it.

SCOPE

This document establishes the roles and responsibilities of Air Force personnel supporting personnel recovery operations and outlines the principles for planning and executing such missions in support of theater campaign objectives. It describes the mission, command relationships, force composition, and planning considerations necessary to conduct operations. It covers basic PRO organization, capabilities, procedures, and the Airman's perspective on joint PR responsibilities. It also discusses the relationship between the Air Force PRO organizations, under the operational control of the commander, Air Force forces (COMAFFOR), and the joint PR agencies.

Ultimately, the JFC and component commanders (Service and functional components) must know and understand their PR duties/responsibilities within the military option of PR. Additionally, they must be able to integrate the military option of PR with the diplomatic and civil options of PR so as to maximize the synergy of an integrated and coordinated PR plan. Commanders must assess each situation independently, consider all PR alternatives, and determine the option best suited to respond to the isolating incident. Due to the vast scope of PR, this document will focus on the Air Force's contribution to the military option of PR.

COMAFFOR / JFACC / CFACC
A note on terminology

One of the cornerstones of Air Force doctrine is "the US Air Force prefers—and in fact, plans and trains—to employ through a COMAFFOR who is also dual-hatted as a JFACC." (AFDD 1)

To simplify the use of nomenclature, Air Force doctrine documents will assume the above case unless specifically stated otherwise. The term "commander, Air Force forces" (COMAFFOR) refers to the Title 10 Service responsibilities while the term "joint force air and space component commander" (JFACC) refers to the joint operational responsibilities.

While both joint and Air Force doctrine state that one individual will normally be dual-hatted as COMAFFOR and JFACC, the two responsibilities are different, and are typically executed through different staffs.

Normally, the COMAFFOR function executes operational control/administrative control of Air Force forces through a Service A-Staff while the JFACC function executes tactical control of all joint air and space component forces through an air and space operations center.

When multinational operations are involved the JFACC becomes a combined forces air and space component commander (CFACC). Likewise, though commonly referred to as an air and space operations center (AOC), in joint or combined operations the correct title is joint air and space operations center (JAOC) or combined air operations center (CAOC).

FOUNDATIONAL DOCTRINE STATEMENTS

Foundational doctrine statements are the basic principles and beliefs upon which AFDDs are built. Other information in the AFDDs expands on or supports these statements.

✪ Air Force personnel recovery operations (PRO) reflect a number of specific tasks performed by Air Force units to recover isolated personnel throughout the entire spectrum of conflict. (Page 1)

✪ Although traditionally PRO assets have focused on the recovery of downed aircrews, recent experiences suggest that Air Force PRO forces are responsible for the recovery of any isolated personnel. (Page 1)

✪ The primary mission of Air Force PRO is to utilize a combination of specially trained Airmen and unique equipment to recover any isolated personnel. (Page 3)

✪ Combat Search and Rescue (CSAR) is how the Air Force accomplishes the PR recovery task. It is the Air Force's preferred mechanism for personnel recovery in uncertain or hostile environments and denied areas. (Page 3)

✪ Although Airmen may place natural emphasis on the recovery of fellow Airmen, Air Force PRO philosophy is based on the assumption that PRO forces must be prepared to recover any isolated personnel anytime, anyplace. (Page 3)

✪ PRO represents the Air Force's coordinated actions and efforts that support the joint PR system, while CSAR is the Air Force's method of choice for accomplishing the recovery task in uncertain, denied, or hostile environments. (Page 10)

✪ There are three CSAR components: the command, control, and coordination node, the recovery forces, and the isolated personnel. (Page 11)

✪ The objective of the CSAR task force is the successful recovery of isolated personnel with no additional loss of friendly assets. (Page 12)

✪ In order to improve mission planning effectiveness, it is optimal to co-locate all dedicated PRO forces. (Page 17)

✪ The COMAFFOR/JFACC should consider the capabilities of the host nation, other Service/functional components, and multinational forces during all phases of PR mission planning. (Page 17)

✪ Early identification of requirements, inclusion in the force enhancement/flexible deterrent option, appropriate PRO priority in the flow of time phased force and deployment data, and frequent reevaluations are keys to sustaining PRO support. (Page 21)

✪ The success of PRO is dependent upon comprehensive education and rigorous training at all levels. (Page 23)

CHAPTER ONE

OVERVIEW

> *...the creed of the enemy. It is a mindset that rejoices in suicide, incites murder, and celebrates every death we mourn. And we who stand on the other side of the line must be equally clear and certain of our convictions. We do love life, the life given to us and to all. We believe in the values that uphold the dignity of life, tolerance, and freedom, and the right of conscience. And we know that this way of life is worth defending.*
>
> **—President George W. Bush**

Before describing the Air Force position on Personnel Recovery Operations (PRO), the reader must understand the joint term "Personnel Recovery" (PR). With Joint Publication 3-50 *Joint Doctrine for Personnel Recovery*, in draft form, the Chairman of the Joint Chiefs of Staff Instruction (CJCSI) 3270.01A, dated July 2004, outlines the most up to date definition of PR. CJCSI 3270.01A defines PR as "the sum of military, diplomatic, and civil efforts to effect the recovery and return of US Military, DOD civilians, and DOD contractor personnel who are isolated or missing while participating in a US government-sanctioned military activity or missions in an uncertain or hostile environment, or as determined by the Secretary of Defense."

CJCSI 3270.01A also defines another key term that must be explained up front. According to CJCSI 3270.01A, isolated personnel (IP) are "US military, DOD civilians, or DOD contractor personnel, or other personnel designated by the President or Secretary of Defense, who have become separated from their unit or organization in an uncertain or hostile environment or denied area, requiring them to survive, evade, or escape." Throughout the rest of this document, the terms PR and isolated personnel are utilized in accordance with CJCSI 3270.01A.

Air Force PRO reflect a number of specific tasks performed by Air Force units to recover isolated personnel throughout the entire spectrum of conflict. The term Airmen refers to all active duty, Air Force Reserve, Air National Guard, and civilian Air Force Personnel. Civilian contractors who work for the Air Force in a combat environment are not considered "Airmen." But they are covered, in terms of PR, under the umbrella term of "isolated personnel."

The Air Force organizes, trains, and equips personnel to conduct PRO using the fastest and most effective means, across the range of military operations. Air Force PRO forces deploy to recover personnel or equipment with specially outfitted aircraft/vehicles, specially trained aircrews and ground recovery teams in response to geographic combatant commander taskings. **Although traditionally PRO assets have focused on the recovery of downed aircrews, recent**

experiences suggest that Air Force PRO forces are responsible for the recovery of any isolated personnel.

The United States government has three options available for recovery of isolated personnel: military, diplomatic, and civil. This doctrine document focuses on the military option. Specifically, it codifies the Air Force's operational level doctrine on PRO and how Air Force PRO complements joint PR concepts.

HISTORICAL PERSPECTIVE

Code of an Air Rescue Man

It is my duty, as a member of the Air Rescue Service, to save life and aid the injured.

I will be prepared at all times to perform my assigned duties quickly and efficiently, placing these duties before personal desires and comforts.

These things I do THAT OTHERS MAY LIVE

—**Brig Gen Richard Kight**
Commander Air Rescue Service, 1 Dec 1946 – 8 Jul 1952

The Air Force has a rich history in the recovery of isolated personnel dating back to the World War II era Army Air Corps (AAC). Heavy combat losses in the European Theater prompted AAC leaders to join efforts with the Royal Air Force Air-Sea Rescue Organization in demonstrating the first US aviation rescue capability. In the Pacific Theater, each unit developed its own rescue capability to meet unique requirements. By 1946, the Army Air Force had consolidated search and rescue operations and training under the Air Rescue Service (ARS). The ARS was re-designated as the Aerospace Rescue and Recovery Service (ARRS) in 1964. During the Vietnam conflict, the ARRS was the most effective combat aircrew recovery force ever, rescuing over 3,800 personnel. After Vietnam, the ARRS established the Air Force Rescue Coordination Center to coordinate inland search and rescue (SAR) in the continental US and began providing missile site support to Strategic Air Command and logistic support to remote Air Force sites. In 1983, ARRS merged with Air Force special operations forces (AFSOF) to form the 23d Air Force under Military Airlift Command (MAC). In 1989, Headquarters Air Rescue

Personnel and machine: Air Force CSAR during Operation Iraqi Freedom

Service was reactivated under MAC. In 1993, the Air Force inactivated the ARS and transferred the air rescue forces to the Air Combat Command (ACC). In 2003, Air Force Special Operations Command (AFSOC) became the lead command for the PRO mission and gained administrative control of continental US (CONUS)-based PRO forces.

MISSIONS

The Air Force organizes, trains, and equips its PRO force to provide unique PR capabilities to combatant commanders. **The primary mission of Air Force PRO is to utilize a combination of specially trained Airmen and unique equipment to recover any isolated personnel.** By virtue of the inherent capabilities of PRO forces, they can accomplish other collateral missions. Historically, these collateral missions have included: casualty evacuation, civil SAR, counter-drug activities, emergency aeromedical evacuation, homeland security, humanitarian relief, international aid, non-combatant evacuation operations, support for National Aeronautics and Space Administration flight operations, infiltration and exfiltration of personnel in support of air component commander missions, and special operations missions, including PR of special operations forces.

COMBAT SEARCH AND RESCUE

Combat Search and Rescue (CSAR) is how the Air Force accomplishes the PR recovery task. It is the Air Force's preferred mechanism for personnel recovery in uncertain or hostile environments and denied areas. Under the PRO construct, CSAR is the way that PRO forces execute the recovery task. Chapter three describes this recovery method in detail. Air Force PRO is only part of the joint PR system. Chapter two briefly explains how PRO fits within the joint architecture.

PRO PHILOSOPHY AND BENEFITS

The Department of Defense has mandated that each Service must maintain a unilateral PR capability in support of its own operations. This responsibility is codified in joint doctrine through the Chairman of the Joint Chiefs of Staff in Joint Publication (JP) 3-50, *Joint Personnel Recovery* (Draft). **Although Airmen may place natural emphasis on the recovery of fellow Airmen, Air Force PRO philosophy is based on the assumption that PRO forces must be prepared to recover any isolated personnel anytime, anyplace.** The successful recovery of isolated personnel is an intangible force multiplier that transcends the tactical to the operational and strategic levels of war. Additionally, PRO is an integral part of US combat operations and must be considered across the range of military operations. It is a key element in sustaining the morale, cohesion, and fighting capability of friendly forces. It preserves critical combat resources and influences the course of national and international politics by denying adversaries the opportunity to exploit the intelligence and propaganda value of captured personnel.

CITATION TO ACCOMPANY THE AWARD OF
THE AIR FORCE CROSS
(POSTHUMOUS)

TO

JASON D. CUNNINGHAM

The President of the United States of America, authorized by Title 10, Section 8742, U.S.C., awards the Air Force Cross to Senior Airman Jason D. Cunningham for extraordinary heroism in military operations against an opposing armed force while serving as a pararescueman near the village of Marzak in the Paktia Province of Afghanistan on 4 March 2002. On that proud day, Airman Cunningham was the primary Air Force Combat Search and Rescue medic assigned to a Quick Reaction Force tasked to recover two American servicemen evading capture in austere terrain occupied by massed Al Qaida and Taliban forces. Shortly before landing, his MH-47E helicopter received accurate rocket-propelled grenade and small arms fire, severely disabling the aircraft and causing it to crash land. The assault force formed a hasty defense and immediately suffered three fatalities and five critical casualties. Despite effective enemy fire, and at great risk to his own life, Airman Cunningham remained in the burning fuselage of the aircraft in order to treat the wounded. As he moved his patients to a more secure location, mortar rounds began to impact within fifty feet of his position. Disregarding this extreme danger, he continued the movement and exposed himself to enemy fire on seven separate occasions. When the second casualty collection point was also compromised, in a display of uncommon valor and gallantry, Airman Cunningham braved an intense small arms and rocket-propelled grenade attack while repositioning the critically wounded to a third collection point. Even after he was mortally wounded and quickly deteriorating, he continued to direct patient movement and transferred care to another medic. In the end, his distinct efforts led to the successful delivery of ten gravely wounded Americans to life-saving medical treatment. Through his extraordinary heroism, superb airmanship, aggressiveness in the face of the enemy, and in the dedication of his service to his country, Senior Airman Cunningham reflected the highest credit upon himself and the United States Air Force.

CHAPTER TWO

PERSONNEL RECOVERY ESSENTIAL TASKS

> *The brave men and women who serve today ... can do so with the full confidence that if they are captured, become missing or fall in battle, this nation will spare no effort to bring them home. This our solemn pledge: however long it takes, whatever it takes, whatever the cost.*
> —**Paul Wolfowitz, Deputy Secretary of Defense, September 2004**

OVERVIEW OF THE JOINT PERSONNEL RECOVERY SYSTEM[1]

While Air Force PRO can collaterally recover isolated personnel (IP) from any Service, DOD Directive 2310.2, *Personnel Recovery*, and legacy JP 3-50 series publications codify that each Service is primarily responsible for the PR coverage of their own operations. Until recently, according to these DOD directives, the Air Force's Service responsibility was to provide for the recovery of Airmen. In short, new directives have expanded the joint PR mission construct greatly. CJCSI 3270.01A commits each Service to the recovery of any captured, missing, or isolated personnel from uncertain or hostile environments and denied areas.

According to CJCSI 3270.01A, *DOD personnel recovery systems exist to ensure a complete and coordinated effort to recover US military, DOD civilians and DOD contractor personnel, and other personnel directed by the President of the United States or Secretary of Defense.* Air Force PRO capabilities, tactics, techniques, and procedures represent an integral part of the joint PR system. This system consists of the *preparation*, *planning*, *execution* and *adaptation* functions. Although the activities within these functions can happen consecutively, they generally occur concurrently or, at a minimum, they overlap in their execution.

Preparation entails activities that commanders, their staffs, PR forces, and Airmen accomplish in order to get ready for a situation that requires PRO. Properly organized, trained, and equipped forces enhance chances of successful recovery. Planning includes the collective efforts of commanders and staffs, PR forces, and isolated personnel to integrate and employ Air Force PRO elements in an effective manner. Adaptation reflects the process of continuous improvement. Lessons learned, assessments, requirements determination, concept development and experimentation, etc., enable forces to adapt to new ideas and concepts in order to accomplish successful PRO. This chapter concentrates on the planning and execution functions. Under the joint PR construct, vital to proper planning and PR execution is familiarity with the joint personnel recovery center (JPRC) concept, and a good understanding of the five essential

---

[1] Information based on JP 3-50, *Joint Personnel Recovery*, draft copy. This section reflects approved concepts regarding the JPRC produced in coordination with the Joint Personnel Recovery Agency (JPRA), the lead proponent for joint PR issues. Also note that JP 3-50 explains JPRC responsibilities in great detail. Since it will be in draft form long after AFDD 2-1.6 is published, this document purposely stays away from JPRC TTP discussions.

PR tasks.[2] Like the joint PR construct, the Air Force PRO concept is centered on five essential tasks: *report, locate, support, recover* and *reintegrate*.

JOINT PERSONNEL RECOVERY CENTER

By direction of the Chairman of the Joint Chiefs of Staff, geographic combatant commanders should establish a standing JPRC or functional equivalent. Joint force commanders (JFCs), who may be combatant commanders, subunified commanders, or joint task force (JTF) commanders, normally designate the responsibility for the joint PR mission area to the joint operations directorate (J-3) or to a component commander. The JPRC is integrated into the appropriate operations center.

If the JFC chooses to coordinate joint PR through a component commander, the JFC should also designate them as *supported commander* for the joint PR mission area. This way, the JFC delegates to the supported commander the necessary authority to successfully accomplish the five PR tasks. This relationship should be evaluated as operations progress through the different campaign phases. For example, while the joint force air component commander (JFACC) may be designated the supported commander for joint PR during major combat operations (often referred to as "Phase III"), but the JFC should reevaluate the support/supporting relationship when the campaign shifts to other phases (e.g., counter-insurgency operations).

At the same time, component commanders have primary authority and responsibility to plan and conduct PR in support of their own operations. In other words, whether the JFC elects to coordinate PR through the J-3 or a component commander, all Service components should maintain a personnel recovery coordination cell (PRCC) capability in order to execute component PR responsibilities. For example, the COMAFFOR should establish a PRCC to coordinate air component PR activities, including coordination with the JPRC and other component PRCCs, as appropriate. The air component PRCC should be collocated with the joint air and space operations center (JAOC) and manned with personnel specifically trained to effectively coordinate joint PR activities.

THE FIVE PERSONNEL RECOVERY OPERATIONS ESSENTIAL TASKS

Report

Awareness and notification initiate the PRO process. Rapid and accurate notification is essential for a successful recovery. Threat conditions permitting, IP should attempt to establish contact with friendly forces IAW notification procedures as outlined in the PR special instructions (SPINS) portion of the air tasking order (ATO).

Initial Response: once an actual or potential PR incident or potential isolating event is observed, the JPRC should be notified immediately through PR communications architecture. In most cases, the JPRC is established at the joint or combined air operations center. Upon

---

[2] Note that the term JPRC replaces the term joint search recovery center (JSRC). Similarly, the term PRCC replaces the legacy rescue coordination center (RCC) term.

notification, the JPRC coordinates with the Air Force PRCC. The PRCC may assume PR mission coordinator responsibilities for missions involving Airmen, but should synchronize the use of PRO forces and other supporting assets through the JPRC. The PRCC or JPRC will notify responding units and brief pertinent aspects of the mission. The response time and operations concept will depend on the enemy threat en route or near the survivor's location, environmental conditions, available assets, and other factors.

Locate

Some of the methods used to locate IP include: theater electronic surveillance, reconnaissance, command and control (C2) aircraft, global satellites, wingman reports, and visual search by PRO forces. PRO forces will most likely employ based on near real time information on the IP's position. Even with precise coordinates that can pinpoint the isolated person's location, PRO forces still have to authenticate the isolated person's identity prior to facilitating successful support and recovery operations.

An effective authentication system is essential to prevent the compromise of vital information and minimize risk to isolated personnel and the recovery force. This holds true because PRO assets are extremely vulnerable during the execution phase and need exact and reliable authentication information. Accordingly, IP and rescue forces should take extreme care not to compromise authentication information and allow its use over an extended period. Some of the ways that PRO forces authenticate isolated personnel in hostile environments, including CSAR/PR code words, letters, numbers, and visual signals, as well as isolated personnel report (ISOPREP) data. Of these, the CSAR/PR codes are the most common means of authentication. Authentication procedures are detailed in the JP 3-50 series publications. Ordinarily, theater or AOR-specific additional procedures are published in appropriate directives, operations plans (OPLANs), and/or PR special instructions (SPINS).

Support

Support is the planned effort necessary to ensure the physical and psychological sustainment of IP. This may include establishing two-way communications, providing morale-building support, aerial resupply, or aerial escort to a cache. Support may also encompass the suppression of enemy threats to the IP. This may preclude capture for the isolated person and disrupt the adversary's response to PRO efforts. When necessary, combat rescue officers/pararescue specialists (CRO/PJs) and/or equipment may be pre-positioned to support the IP until the recovery phase. Besides support to the IP, this task includes physical and psychological assistance to the IP's family.

Support measures begin before and after an individual becomes isolated. This support is manifested in the theater PR SPINS, home-station arrangements and training prior to entry in to a specific theater, theater PR regulations, and the establishment of the theater PR architecture. All of these are component responsibilities that frame the support mechanism.

Recover

This task reflects activities by commanders, staff, recovery force, and IP to physically recover the IP. This includes the planning as well as execution phases. CSAR is the Air Force's preferred recovery mechanism. As information of a potential PR incident becomes available, the PRCC should assess the situation quickly, determine mission feasibility, and disseminate data to units that may participate in the rescue mission. Once mission execution appears feasible, units may be tasked to initiate/continue planning or launch from alert. If they launch, the recovery force will include PRO and all the necessary supporting forces required to execute a recovery operation.

Only the JFC or his/her designated supported commander for PR can issue the "execution order." Based on the JFC's guidance, the JFACC will direct PRO assets to conduct the recovery of the IP. The execution authority is granted in accordance with theater PR concept of operations/standard operating procedures/SPINS and may be pre-arranged in some situations and for certain missions. Once the JFACC gives the launch authority, the recovery and rescue forces proceed to the isolated personnel location and execute the recovery. Although the tactical level issues are beyond the scope of this document, at the operational level, the JFC or his designated supported commander for PR normally retains execution authority at that level.

By their very nature, PROs are time-sensitive undertakings. According to numerous historical studies, after four or more hours on the ground, the chance that a survivor in combat will be successfully rescued is historically less than twenty percent. Ideally, PRO will be able to bring the isolated personnel under the control of the recovery force in less than two hours; this is a goal, not a strict requirement.

Although the Air Force's preferred PR mechanism is described in detail in chapter three, generally there are two types of PR response postures: from alert and deliberate.

Alert

Immediate response missions commence from a dedicated ground or airborne alert posture. In order to decrease flight time to the anticipated recovery area and reduce air refueling requirements, rescue forces may be located on the ground at a forward location or loitering in anticipation of an execution order. Additionally, these forces may be embedded in existing airborne missions to further reduce response time.

Deliberate

Like the launch from alert, this recovery posture requires knowledge of the location of the isolated personnel. But unlike alert launches, commanders choose this method when an immediate response may not be possible due to environmental, political, or threat considerations. Deliberately planned missions give planners the flexibility to utilize all necessary assets to complete the recovery.

Reintegrate

The reintegration task begins when the recovery force relinquishes physical control of previously isolated personnel to a designated team member or organization in the theater reintegration process. As part of reintegration, PRO forces collect perishable essential intelligence and survival, evasion, resistance, escape (SERE) information, while at the same time tending to the physical and psychological welfare of recovered isolated personnel. The welfare portion of the reintegration process may be a long-term endeavor with no specific end date.

Ultimately, theater reintegration procedures are based on DOD Instruction 2310.4, *Repatriation of Prisoners of War (POW) Hostages, Peacetime Governmental Detainees and Other Missing or Isolated Personnel*, and reflect the combatant commanders' commitment to return isolated personnel to duty or their unit in the most expeditious and healthiest manner possible.

CHAPTER THREE

AIR FORCE COMBAT SEARCH AND RESCUE (CSAR): THE RECOVERY MECHANISM

PRO represents the Air Force's coordinated actions and efforts that support the joint PR system, while CSAR is the Air Force's method of choice for accomplishing the recovery task in uncertain, denied, or hostile environments. The Air Force organizes, trains, and equips unique forces that focus specifically on PRO. When PRO assets cannot avoid the threat on their own, a myriad of other assets can be employed to protect the recovery forces thereby permitting the PRO to proceed with the best chance of success.

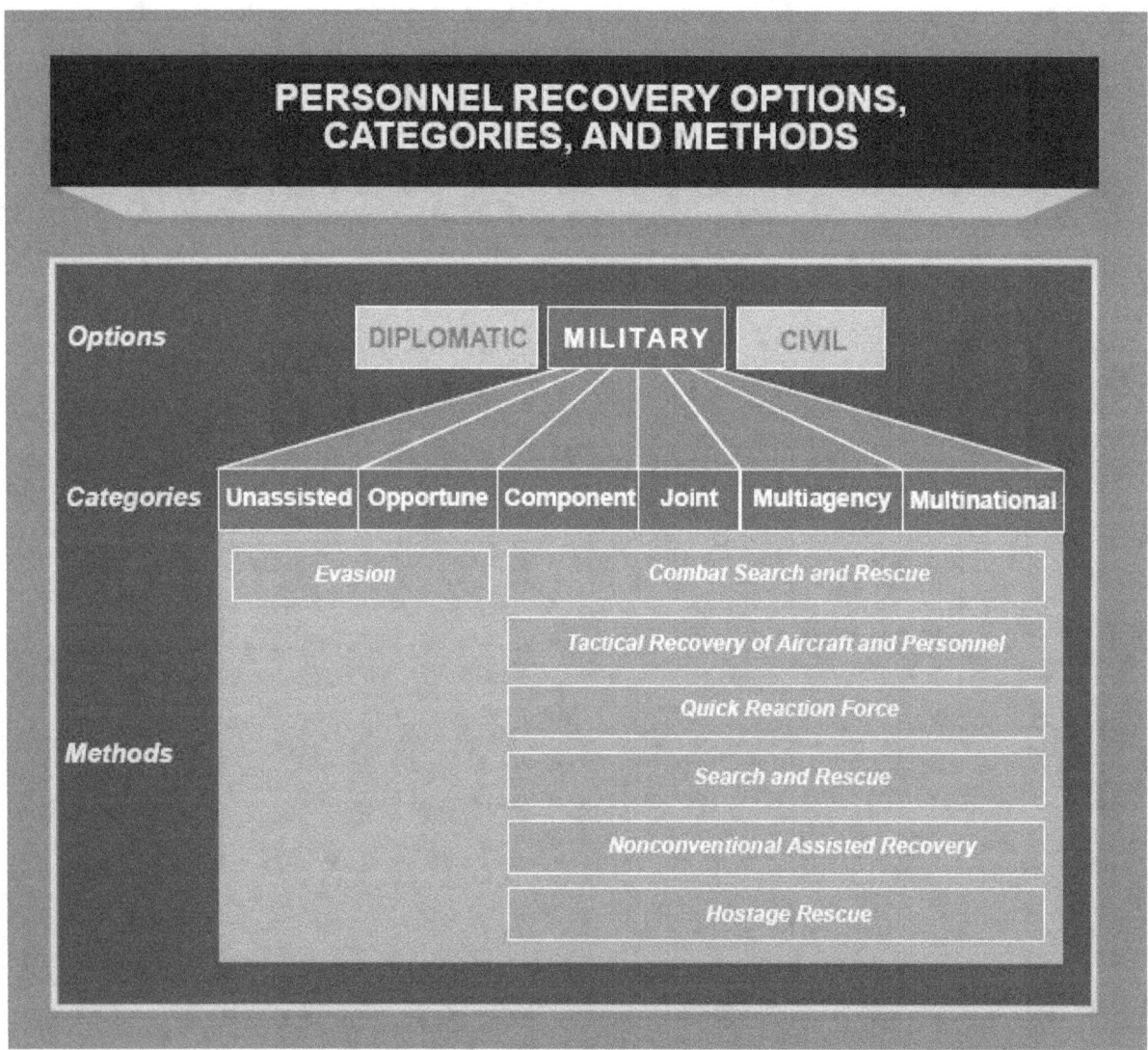

Figure 3.1. CSAR represents the Air Force's method of choice for PR in denied or hostile environment.

CSAR COMPONENTS

There are three CSAR components: the command, control, and coordination node; the recovery forces; and the isolated personnel. The PRCC allows the JFACC to command/control and coordinate PRO force activities with the JPRC and other components. The second component represents the dedicated Air Force assets that organize, train, and perform personnel recovery operations and are the most likely assets that often augment PRO forces. The Air Force normally employs recovery forces under the CSAR task force (CSARTF) concept, explained later in this chapter. Although the CSARTF is not limited to the Air Force assets only, this publication's scope is authoritative only to Air Force personnel. The final component of CSAR is the most vital element of the PR construct: the isolated personnel.

In short, the following sections describe the CSAR capabilities, the Air Force's preferred mechanism for PRO. Again, Air Force PRO is a key element of the greater PR concept. CSAR is the recovery mechanism employed by the Air Force to accomplish the "Recover" task of the five joint PR tasks. Combining properly organized, trained, and equipped rotary-/fixed-wing forces and PRO ground elements, the Air Force is well postured to recover any isolated personnel in a variety of environments.

COMMAND, CONTROL, AND COORDINATION

Personnel Recovery Coordination Cell (PRCC)

The Air Force component's PRCC is the hub of Air Force PRO activities and is typically located in the JAOC. Air Force units will report all isolating incidents to the PRCC. Even if the JFACC is designated the supported commander for PR, the JFACC should maintain a PRCC capability in order to tend to air component PR responsibilities. The PRCC responsibilities include:

✪ Initiating and monitoring PRO planning.

✪ Maintaining real time intelligence information on systems posing threats to PROs.

✪ Designating ISOPREP control points.

✪ Obtaining ISOPREP data and evasion plans of action (EPAs) from units.

✪ Coordinating tasking among Air Force PRO-capable forces.

✪ Informing the JPRC if JFACC forces are capable of executing the mission.

✪ Requesting additional recovery forces through the JPRC if Air Force PRO forces are unable to execute the PR mission unilaterally.

✪ Coordinating PRO activities with the JPRC, supporting agencies, medical representatives, a variety of other government and non-government agencies, and the requesting unit.

✪ Distributing PR SPINS to the JFACC's subordinate units. Note that the PRCC is still responsible for coordination of PR SPINS with other component commands and the JPRC.

The PRCC is also responsible for reviewing and developing PR appendices to Annex C (Operations) for air component supporting OPLANs, concept plans, and operational orders. Key duty positions inside the PRCC are explained below.

Director, Personnel Recovery Coordination Cell

The JFACC directs Air Force CSAR operations through the PRCC director who is responsible for the day-to-day operations of the PRCC. If the JFACC is designated the supported commander responsible for joint PR operations, the PRCC director will normally be dual-hatted as the PRCC and JPRC director.

Personnel Recovery Plans Officer

The personnel recovery operations plans officer (PRPO) ordinarily works in the AOC's combat plans division, participates in the master air attack plan (MAAP) development, and carefully integrates PRO assets into the MAAP in order to minimize potential recovery time of IP. Once PRO is incorporated in the MAAP, the PRPO provides PRO planning inputs for the ATO production.

Personnel Recovery Duty Officer

The personnel recovery operations duty officer (PRDO) ordinarily works in the AOC's combat operations division and coordinates real-time support for PRO. The PRDO monitors ATO changes and is responsible for PRO specific ATO matters until the ATO is "pushed" to the combat operations floor. Since PRO assets normally require support from other forces to conduct recovery operations, the PRDO coordinates this real-time support with the other duty officers on the combat operations floor of the AOC (i.e., senior operations duty officer [SODO] and fighter duty officer [FODO]).

RECOVERY FORCES

Since the Vietnam War, Air Force personnel recovery efforts have been combined into a tailored CSARTF – a proven mechanism that has significantly enhanced CSAR operations. The size and complexity of the CSARTF has depended on the mission requirements and the threat.

A CSARTF is a mutually supporting package of assets tailored to meet a specific CSAR requirement. **The objective of the CSARTF is the successful recovery of isolated personnel with no additional loss of friendly assets.** The exact composition of the CSARTF varies with the threats en route to, from, and in the vicinity of the isolated personnel. With proper planning, the CSARTF will be able to defeat or degrade the threat to an acceptable level of risk and enable the successful recovery of the IP.

Due to changing threat conditions and/or IP status en route to the objective, the CSARTF may require numerous adjustments and further augmentation during recovery operations. As such, all of the JFACC's aircraft should be prepared to be re-tasked to assist recovery operations.

Additionally, the PRCC must be prepared to request augmentation and support from the other functional/service components through the JPRC.

The CSARTF had two distinct elements: PRO dedicated assets and other augmenting assets. Dedicated forces include rotary- and fixed-wing aircraft, specially trained "battlefield Airmen," and specific duty positions crucial in the PRO execution.

PRO Dedicated Forces

Vertical-lift Aircraft

PRO helicopters are utilized for long range, low level, day/night marginal weather operations into hostile environments to recover distressed or isolated personnel. Missions may be flown in single-ship or multi-ship formations. Similarly, they may be employed as part of a large composite force (e.g., embedded in a large strike air package) or launched in response to a PR situation. The HH-60G is the premier PRO helicopter. Note, however, that vertical-lift assets would include both helicopters and tilt-rotor aircraft. As tilt-rotor aircraft are introduced into the Air Force inventory, some of the lines between traditional rotary- and fixed-wing aircraft may be blurred as technological advancements create leaps in PRO capabilities. AFSOF vertical-lift aircraft maintain comparable PR capabilities. Capabilities wise, AFSOF and PRO forces complement each other well.

Fixed-Wing Rescue Aircraft

Fixed-wing rescue assets are another key element of PRO. Their primary role is to extend the operational range of PRO helicopters. The depth of the battlespace and isolated personnel's location may require that helicopter refueling be conducted in a non-permissive environment. Besides aerial refueling, these assets are capable of airdropping or airlanding recovery teams and/or equipment to assist and/or recover isolated personnel. Additionally, fixed-wing rescue aircraft have an expanded communications capability, making them a natural communication relay platform, and their extended range allows movement of recovered IP over longer distances. The HC-130P is the premier PRO fixed-wing platform. AFSOF fixed-wing aircraft maintain comparable PR capabilities. Again, from a capabilities perspective, AFSOF and PRO forces complement each other well.

Recovery Teams

Air Force recovery teams (RT) are part of the GUARDIAN ANGEL weapon system. GUARDIAN ANGEL is an Air Force human/equipment based weapon system that provides the ground element of the PRO forces and is designed to assist in the execution of all five tasks of PR (Report, Locate, Support, Recover & Reintegrate). RT may have to deploy into uncertain or hostile environments and denied areas prior to, during, and after combat operations in support of the JFC's comprehensive PR plan.

RT consist of CRO, PJ, and SERE specialists. These forces are specially trained to develop theater PR special instructions and conduct PR operations. On the one hand,

CRO/SERE specialists provide specific expertise in the report, locate, support, and reintegrate tasks when attached to operational squadrons, component PRCC, or the theater JPRC. On the other hand, CRO/PJs provide the critical air to ground link between airborne rescue platforms and isolated personnel.

SERE personnel are responsible to provide theater-specific SERE information and develop and facilitate advanced PR training in support of unique contingency requirements. SERE specialists serve as the component/unit level focal point for SERE activities throughout the assigned area of responsibility.

CRO/PJs may assist in recovery efforts as separate surface elements or as part of an aircrew. In other words, CRO/PJs may operate independently or in conjunction with rotary- and fixed-wing aircraft, watercraft, and overland vehicles. In this capacity, CRO/PJs locate, authenticate, provide support via ground threat suppression protection, provide medical aid, offer assistance during evasion, and perform CSAR operations that include transportation of IP from locations inaccessible to recovery vehicles. Team composition and requirements are developed during mission planning and are based on the best available intelligence assessment of the enemy and the condition/location of the IP.

The GUARDIAN ANGEL is the premier personnel recovery ground team. AFSOF special tactics teams maintain comparable capability to execute the recovery task. Again, from a capabilities perspective, AFSOF and PRO forces complement each other well.

Rescue Mission Commander (RMC)

The RMC is a distinct qualification for Airmen specifically trained in CSAR tactics, techniques, and procedures (TTP). RMC responsibilities include establishing communications, locating and authenticating the IP, and protecting the IP until recovery assets arrive. The RMC controls all assets assigned to the PR effort; including, but not limited to, rescue combat air patrol (RESCAP), suppression of enemy air defenses (SEAD), additional strike aircraft, and required aerial refueling.

Rescue Escort (RESCORT)

Based on threats to the IP and the recovery force, rescue escort (RESCORT) is an integral part of CSARTF. RESCORT aircraft provide navigation assistance, route sanitization, and armed escort for the recovery vehicle(s). In increased threat environments, this assistance significantly improves the chances of a successful recovery.

Ideally, RESCORT aircraft should be tactical aircraft capable of operating in the same environment as recovery vehicles. RESCORT formations must be proficient in rendezvous procedures, escort tactics at medium and low altitudes, and defense of the rescue vehicles during mission execution. In the hands of CSAR-qualified pilots, the A-10 is considered the premier RESCORT platform, based on the unique aircraft performance and capabilities. Additionally, CSAR qualified F-16, F-15E, F-18, AV-8 and AC-130 aircraft may be utilized in lieu of A-10s. Rotary-wing escort, such as AH-64, AH-1 and MH-60L may be utilized as well.

Airborne Mission Coordinator (AMC)

An AMC coordinates the flying mission for forces designated to support a specific CSAR operation. The AMC may be designated by component PRCCs or higher authority to coordinate the efforts of several assets. The AMC serves as an airborne communications and data relay between rescue forces and command elements. The E-3 Airborne Warning and Control System (AWACS), though heavily tasked, is the most capable AMC platform due to its extensive communications capability and ability to oversee the air picture. Other multi-crewed assets such as the Navy E-2 Hawkeye, and the E-8 joint surveillance, target attack radar system (JSTARS) are also acceptable AMC platforms.

On-scene Commander (OSC)

The OSC is the individual who initiates rescue efforts in the objective area until rescue forces arrive. Initially, the OSC may be any aircraft in the vicinity, including the wingman of a downed aircraft. The OSC's initial actions are to attempt to establish communication, locate and authenticate the IP, and pass essential elements of information to the AMC. The OSC role will be transferred to the RMC or lead recovery vehicle upon arrival. After transferring OSC duties to the RMC, the original OSC may remain on station in a supporting role.

Additional Augmenting Assets

Forward Air Controller (Airborne) (FAC [A])

The FAC (A) controls air strikes in close proximity to the IP. A FAC (A) may be able to locate and authenticate the isolated personnel before the arrival of other elements of the CSARTF and may be able to function as the OSC until the rescue forces arrive. The FAC (A) may perform OSC duties until the RMC arrives on station. The FAC (A) may also provide a current and accurate assessment of enemy activity in and around the objective area.

Air Refueling Aircraft

Multiple refuelings of both fixed- and vertical-lift aircraft may be required during prolonged CSAR operations. Sequencing of assets between refueling and marshalling points must be carefully managed in order to have all rescue elements available at mission execution time. For real-time CSAR execution, refueling support requirements are relayed through the AMC to the PRCC. The PRCC will orchestrate air refueling support with the tanker coordination cell.

Intelligence, Surveillance, and Reconnaissance (ISR) Platforms

ISR platforms, whether aircraft- or space-based, possess a tremendous capability for supporting CSAR efforts, especially for detecting and locating isolated personnel, as well as monitoring threat systems in the objective area. These assets are also suited to maintaining a listening watch on isolated personnel frequencies when an immediate recovery is not possible. Ultimately, these platforms provide commanders and PRO forces with the situational awareness to make the necessary decisions for the successful recovery of the IP.

Space Systems

In addition to space ISR assets briefly mentioned above, other space systems provide vital communications between the CSARTF, PRO forces, and IP. Additionally, space systems enable precise navigation signals during search and recovery operations.

Suppression of Enemy Air Defenses (SEAD)

SEAD forces minimize the surface-to-air threat to friendly forces executing a PR mission. The F-16CJ and the EA-6B are the premier SEAD platforms. Integrated and interoperable communications between SEAD forces, rescue forces, and ISR platforms are critical. When assigning SEAD platforms the threat environment must be defined for all rescue forces.

Joint and/or Coalition PR Forces

Other Services and/or coalition partners may assist in the PR of isolated Airmen just as Air Force PRO forces assist in the recovery of the joint or coalition personnel. Joint, Service, allied, and foreign publications govern how these forces are integrated within the PR architecture. Nonetheless, it is important, to keep in mind that the Air Force PRO construct is part of a greater PR concept and that Airmen need to work closely with joint and coalition partners to recover any isolated personnel from hostile or uncertain environments and denied areas.

Isolated Personnel

The third component of the Air Force PRO capabilities are the IP who may become stranded in uncertain or hostile environments and denied areas. Although the first two legs of the triad receive extensive specialized training to perform this mission, there is no guarantee that the IP will be trained to PR standards. Since it is up to each Service to provide SERE training to their Soldiers, Sailors, Airmen, Marines, and civilian support personnel, the Air Force can only guarantee the training of Airmen. After all, isolated personnel are the most vital link of the recovery chain.

The task of supporting IP includes equipping, pre-deployment training and contingency planning to ensure that potential IP are fully prepared to adapt to and succeed in isolation, evasion, capture/detainment, recovery, and reintegration. The Air Force properly equips, trains, and familiarizes potential isolated Airmen with PR concepts of operations and procedures in order to facilitate expedient and successful recoveries. Ultimately, the potential for successful PR is significantly improved when IP are trained to joint PR standard. Nonetheless, because not all IP are trained properly, Air Force PRO forces must be ready to recover any personnel, as directed by the Secretary of Defense and the President, regardless of their training in PR procedures.

CHAPTER FOUR

PRO PLANNING AND MOBILITY SUPPORT CONSIDERATIONS

> *Of course, we couldn't start anything until CSAR [force] was in place, so let's talk about getting the CSAR in place.*
>
> **—General Richard Myers, CJCS, to Secretary Donald Rumsfeld**
> ***Bush At War*, Bob Woodward**

PLANNING SUPPORT CONSIDERATIONS

General Planning Considerations

The specific information required for premission planning and for execution/launch authority includes such items as the location of IP, authentication, threat/weather/terrain assessment, and evaluation of safe passage corridors, and air refueling capabilities. **In order to improve mission planning effectiveness, it is optimal to co-locate all dedicated PRO forces.** Also, direct communication with the JAOC, the JPRC, PRCCs, and wing operations centers is essential. This direct communication is most important when the battlefield conditions dictate the formation of a robust CSARTF.

Additionally, **the JFACC should consider the capabilities of the host nation, other Service/functional components, and multinational forces during all phases of PR mission planning.** Accordingly, PRO should be thoroughly integrated in deliberate mission planning and considered as early as possible in crisis action planning.

The dynamic nature of PRO creates the need to fully integrate PR considerations in the MAAP in order to ensure maximum flexibility and responsiveness for PRO forces on the ATO. PRO should be coordinated throughout the CAOC and with other component liaisons, to include: the battlefield coordination detachment (BCD), naval liaison element (NALE), special operations liaison element (SOLE), marine liaisons (MARLO), aeromedical evacuation element, combat operations/plans directorates, airspace, etc.

As part of the planning process, Air Force personnel conducting and supporting PROs must be thoroughly familiar with the laws of armed conflict (LOAC) and applicable rules of engagement (ROE). This is particularly important when addressing issues of the use of force during CSAR operations (to include self-defense considerations), as well as treatment and release of persons captured or detained. LOAC application during low-intensity operations may be complicated by organizational structures, responsibilities, and status of potential adversaries. Only extensive LOAC training can provide PRO forces the proper foundation that enables sound judgment in ambiguous situations.

Another key concept that enables successful recovery operations, while properly adhering to LOAC, is clear and consistent ROE. PRO forces must attempt to influence the ROE development process as early as possible, in order to gain maximum flexibility in recovering isolated personnel throughout the spectrum of conflict.

Similarly, commanders must ensure that operational risk management (ORM) is considered early on in the planning process and integrated throughout all phases of an operation. This way the commander ensures that limited PRO assets are not misused. Potential hazards must be identified and prioritized, and mitigation options assessed so that commanders can make informed risk decisions at the appropriate level. During each PR incident, the ORM process should allow the commander to weigh the level of risk against the potential for success, thus ensuring the most effective and efficient use of PRO assets.

Communications

Rapid, reliable, and secure flow of information is a key factor that contributes to PR success. The JPRC and the Air Force's three CSAR components (PRCC, the recovery forces, and IP) should be able to communicate over long distances, with minimum of interference or intrusion, and with low probability of detection or interception. JPRCs and PRCCs should have access to dedicated communication systems that provide redundant capabilities for secure inter- and intra-theater data and voice transmission. Proper planning, coordination, and brevity optimize the use of communications systems. Communication planning requires integrating theater, component, and unit operating instructions and execution checklists. Successful contact procedures require thoroughly developed and coordinated planning, established contact procedures, and timely execution. The importance of good communications between isolated personnel and rescue forces cannot be overstressed. Communications-out procedures, or procedures for handling situations when communications are disrupted, or personnel/units are unexpectedly out of contact, are often warranted but should be commensurate with the enemy's signal intelligence capability. Brevity words and terminology can be found in Air Force Tactics, Techniques, and Procedures (AFTTP) 3-1, Volume 1, theater directives, and tasking orders. The PRO plan must provide adequate redundancy to compensate in case of equipment or communications failure during any phase of mission execution.

Intelligence

Successful PRO require timely and accurate intelligence support. Intelligence support is always an integral part of PRO. As such, intelligence specialists should be assigned to, and deploy with, PRCCs and operational rescue units. Due to the flexible nature of PRO, the JPRC, PRCC, and PRO units should have dedicated intelligence specialists who have completed the Joint Personnel Recovery Agency's Intelligence Support to Personnel Recovery course.

A thorough understanding of the geography, enemy order of battle, the local population's social and political attitudes, enemy TTP, as well as friendly order of battle is imperative in all combat operations. But considering the dynamic nature of PR, these factors make intelligence products especially significant in PRO. Based on this information, the JFC, JPRC, JFACC,

PRCC, and PRO units decide whether or not to commit PRO assets, consider tactics and recovery force composition, and coordinate support requirements.

Threat analysis, targeting, collection management, and order-of-battle data must be thoroughly integrated in PRO mission planning. Due to PROs' rapid-response requirements during the recovery phase, however, the CSARTF may have to launch with incomplete threat information. Under these circumstances, intelligence specialists make the full use of intelligence assessments, automated data processing, and mission-planning systems that interface with intelligence databases, in order to provide the most up-to-date threat information to PRO forces.

Security

Information and operations security (OPSEC) are also critical to PRO. Security of information is vital to PRO forces from initial planning stages through execution and even after mission completion. OPSEC denies the enemy information about friendly capabilities and intentions, including advance notice of mission unique training, joint preparations, deployment, and employment. PRO forces can maintain OPSEC by carefully identifying, controlling, and protecting indicators and actions associated with the operation. Failure to implement an effective OPSEC program could result in mission compromise and loss of personnel and resources.

Information Operations

As defined in AFDD 2-5, *Information Operations*, information operations (IO) serve to amplify the effects of traditional military operations. PRO can influence IO planning in four primary ways: First, PR operations return isolated personnel to friendly control, allowing them to fight again. Second, PR operations often influence the course of national and international politics by denying adversaries the opportunity to exploit the intelligence and propaganda value of captured personnel. Third, the presence of a robust and viable CSAR force increases morale, with a resultant increase in operational performance. Finally, PRO contributes to the IO campaign by countering the adversary's deception efforts.

For example, if enemy forces have already captured IP, they may try to deceive PRO forces in order to lure them into an ambush. Even if IP have not been captured, the enemy may try to provide false data to PRO forces and, at the same time, move additional air defense assets into the area in an attempt to ambush the recovery force.

While friendly force communications discipline and adherence to PRO standard operating procedures may counter enemy deception operations, it is important to emphasize that PR operations' success or failure can impact the JFC's information operations (IO) campaign significantly. Ultimately, PRO planners must appreciate the influence of PR operations well beyond the actual recovery of the isolated person. Similarly, IO planners must keep in mind the intrinsic value of PR operations to an IO campaign. PRO and IO planners must work together to maximize the influence of successful PRO and minimize the impact of mission failure.

Medical

Due to the variety of injuries to IP, medical personnel should be integrated into planning, deployment, and support of PRO. The PRCC is the focal point for PRO force coordination with military medical facilities in order to provide medical advice beyond the expertise of the recovery team.

Space Requirements

Air Force PRO forces require timely, accurate, and current space products and support during all phases of PRO, from initial planning through deployment and execution. PRO forces must work closely with integrated space support to determine the most appropriate space products necessary to complete the mission, and forward requirements through established channels to space-derived information and services suppliers. Product requirements can be obtained via the space operations officer in the AOC's combat operations division.

Weather, Illumination, and Topological Considerations

Air Force PRO forces require timely and accurate weather support during all phases of planning, deployment, employment, and redeployment. This allows PRO forces to use weather conditions to their advantage. Temperature, barometric pressure, precipitation, humidity, ground and low-level flight visibility, predicted winds, fog, cloud cover, radio frequency propagation, sensor detection ranges, and other hazards to recovery forces and the IP greatly impact PRO planning and execution.

PRO forces are capable of conducting operations in a wide range of topographical environments. Terrain features often determine the type of PRO capabilities required to conduct recovery operations. Additionally, sunrise, sunset, moonrise, moon phase, predicted ambient light, and hydrographic data affect PRO significantly. These conditions play an important role in the PRO timing and tempo and should be considered critical planning factors for PROs.

MOBILITY SUPPORT CONSIDERATIONS

Early identification of requirements, inclusion in the force enhancement/flexible deterrent option (FE/FDO), appropriate PRO priority in the flow of time phased force and deployment data (TPFDD), and frequent reevaluation are keys to sustaining PRO support. Historically, during contingencies, PR requirements are often an afterthought rather than a preplanned consideration of the joint operation planning and execution system. Similar to air tasking order (ATO) planners, PR action officers on a JFC's staff and PRO officers at the JFACC level should consider PR requirements in conjunction with other operational requirements when developing OPLANs, operations orders (OPORD), FE/FDO and/or TPFDD, etc. For additional information on combat support requirements see AFDD 2-4, *Combat Support*. For TPFDD information, consult Air Force Policy Directive 10-4, *Operations Planning: Air & Space Expeditionary Force Presence Policy*, Capabilities Allocation Annex, and the Air Force Wartime Unit Type Code Summary statements.

Deployment

Air Force PRO forces should have the ability to execute time-sensitive deployments and to deploy as deliberately planned elements of an air and space expeditionary task force (AETF). PRO forces should consider the following deployment factors:

PRO forces should deploy in theater prior to the start of hostilities and be prepared to provide immediate PRO mission capability with minimal support airlift. Tailored rapid-response deployment packages support the intent of the AETF concept and follow-on in-theater contingency operations.

The initial deployment of PR forces in support of Operation ENDURING FREEDOM (OEF) represents a perfect example of the significant emphasis that combatant commanders and Service chiefs put on PR. Military commanders delayed decisive operations until the JFC established an adequate PR capability. Another way to look at this, OEF demonstrated the need to have PR forces in place prior to commencement of combat operations. Based on OEF and other historical data, the PR forces should be listed high on the combatant commander's time phased force deployment list (TPFDL).

Operating Locations

Air Force planners should determine beddown locations for PRO forces based on factors including response time, operations tempo, force protection, and other variables. Recent PROs suggest that support and deployment concepts should include the capability to operate from main operating bases, forward operating bases, forward operating locations, and afloat staging bases for rotary wing assets. Planners should tailor logistical support requirements based on the most likely operating location. To decrease response time and improve the chances of a successful recovery, PRO forces should be positioned as far forward as the situation allows. As an initial planning consideration, the JFACC should have the ability to deploy PRO assets to bare bases and austere environments for up to 14 days with minimum base operating support (BOS).

Main Operating Base (MOB). A base established in friendly territory to provide sustained command and control, administration, and logistical support to PRO activities in designated areas. MOBs provide significant levels of BOS, a well-organized and extensive logistical support organization, and a robust communications infrastructure that enables the recovery forces' access to battlefield C2 and ISR information. If the MOB is significantly removed from the PRO objective area, planners should consider the establishment of airborne alert PRO holding areas, in order to expedite recovery operations.

Forward Operating Base (FOB). An airfield used to support tactical operations without establishing full support facilities. Support from a MOB may be required if PRO forces operate out of an FOB for an extended amount of time.

Forward Operating Locations (FOL). Under these conditions, PRO forces should be able to maintain alert status at FOLs. Almost all support for FOLs will have to come from FOB/MOBs.

For vertical-lift PRO forces, an FOL may or may not be an airfield; it may be a forward arming and refueling point. FOL capability requires, as a minimum, organic communication packages to provide the necessary C2 and ISR for successful mission execution. Again, it is important to understand that for FOL operations, fuel, ammunition, medical supplies, and other mission essential material will have to come from FOBs or MOBs.

Afloat Staging Base (AFSB) Operations. When land-based MOBs, FOBs, or FOLs are unavailable, AFSB operations offer a unique alternative. Although AFSB operations do not require extensive host nation coordination, environmental conditions and the intricacies of shipboard operations offer unique challenges. JP 3.04.1, *Joint Tactics, Techniques, and Procedures for Shipboard Operations*, details requirements for shipboard operations.

CHAPTER FIVE

TRAINING AND EDUCATION

> *War is not an affair of chance. A great deal of knowledge, study, and meditation is necessary to conduct it well.*
>
> —**Frederick the Great**

GENERAL

PRO success is rooted in comprehensive education and rigorous training of commanders and their staff, PRO forces, and isolated personnel. These are key elements of the joint PR adaptation process. In the unit and at specialized schools, realistic "train as you fight" experiences provide the necessary skills to master the five essential tasks of PR.

COMMANDERS AND STAFF

Commanders and staff should take an active role in evaluating local training programs to ensure aircrew training and proficiency levels meet combat readiness requirements. They should also ensure that unit PRO training programs support joint PR interoperability concepts, are integrated with other forces, and that training and exercise programs are realistic and effective.

Flight discipline, crew coordination, mission planning, and mutual support of participating PR forces are essential to effective Air Force PRO force employment. The JP 3-50 series, this document, applicable multi-Service, and AFTTP documents provide a background for developing these fundamentals. Commanders should ensure PRO aircrews, planners, and support personnel are thoroughly familiar with the principles outlined in these documents and can apply them at the operational and tactical level.

PRO FORCES

Training of PRO forces includes: initial qualification training, mission qualification, currency requirements, upgrade training, proficiency, specialized mission certification training, threat training and specialized training. Additionally, beyond unilateral Air Force PRO training, PRO personnel should conduct regularly scheduled joint exercises in order to better integrate with the rest of the joint PR community.

ISOLATED PERSONNEL

Since each Service is responsible to provide SERE training to its own Soldiers, Sailors, Airmen, Marines, and civilian support personnel, the Air Force can only guarantee the training of its own personnel. This AFDD is authoritative for Airmen. In this sense, prior to deployment or immediately after entering a particular theater, Airmen should have the appropriate training that familiarizes them with PR/SERE TTPs, PR SPINS, SOPs, etc. Airmen and high-risk-of-isolation personnel receive additional training as outlined in DOD Directive 1300.7, *Training and Education to Support the Code of Conduct*, and DOD Instruction 1300.21, *Code of Conduct Training and Education*. Additionally, certain theater entry requirements may apply.

The Air Force coordinates with the JPRA, the proponent for joint PR matters, to ensure that there is coordination between Services in terms of PR training and education, as well as a common DOD standard for joint PR procedures. For more information, review AFTTP (Interservice) 3-2.26, *Survival, Evasion, and Recovery: Multi-Service Procedures for Survival, Evasion, and Recovery*, and Air Force Manual (AFM) 36-2216, Vol I & II, *SERE Mobile Operations*.

PERSONNEL RECOVERY COORDINATION CELL PERSONNEL

PRCC personnel must complete the AOC initial qualification training for PR and other applicable JPRA PR courses, such as the joint personnel recovery coordinators course. Additionally, all PRCC personnel should complete local orientation training tailored to the specific AOC that they are being assigned to. Other courses, such as the Inland SAR and Maritime SAR courses taught by the Coast Guard, and the Air Force joint doctrine air campaign course, are strongly encouraged. In fact, any courses that teach development of air campaign plans and the integration of PROs under the joint and interagency PR umbrella are strongly encouraged.

EXERCISES

To ensure interoperability, Air Force PRO staffs and forces should exercise regularly with augmentation personnel and forces. These training evolutions should exercise the system as a whole, including the JFACC, AOC, PRCC, elements of the CSARTF, AMC, OSC, RMC, and the IP. For example, Joint Chiefs of Staff field training exercises (FTX) and combat air forces (CAF) FLAG exercises facilitate the integration of joint forces in realistic scenarios that stress the entire joint PR system.

Independently, the COMAFFOR should conduct AOC exercises that emphasize command, control, communications, and intelligence coordination procedures. These exercises provide important experience for PRCC personnel, which is normally not available during FTX participation. The CAF exercises include both active duty and air reserve component forces.

The Air Force PRO construct is part of a greater PR concept; Airmen need to work closely with joint and Coalition partners to recovery any isolated personnel from hostile or uncertain environments and denied areas. Therefore, joint and combined training can enable interoperability and improve integration between Air Force PRO forces and their joint/combined partners.

SUGGESTED READINGS

Air Force Publications (Note: All Air Force doctrine documents are available on the Air Force Doctrine Center web page at **https://www.doctrine.af.mil**)

AFDD 1, *Air Force Basic Doctrine*

AFDD 2, *Organization and Employment of Air and Space Operations*

AFDD 2-1, *Air Warfare*

AFDD 2-4, *Combat Support*

AFDD 2-5, *Information Operations*

AFDD 2-7, *Air Force Special Operations*

Air Force Manual (AFM) 36-2216, Vol I & II, *SERE Mobile Operations*

AFTTP (I) 3-2.26, *Survival, Evasion, and Recovery: Multi-Service Procedures for Survival, Evasion, and Recovery* (available at https://wwwmil.alsa.mil/surv.htm)

Air Force Policy Directive 10-4, *Operations Planning: Air & Space Expeditionary Force Presence Policy*, Capabilities Allocation Annex and the Air Force Wartime UTC Summary statements

Joint Publications

JP 0-2, *Unified Action Armed Forces (UNAAF)*

JP 3-50, *Joint Doctrine for Personnel Recovery*, (Draft)

JP 3-50.2, *Doctrine for Joint Combat Search and Rescue*

JP 3-50.21, *Joint Tactics, Techniques and Procedures for Combat Search and Rescue*

JP 3-50.3, *Joint Doctrine for Evasion and Recovery*

Other Publications

Brehm, Jack with Pete Nelson, *That Others May Live: The True Story of a PJ, a Member of America's Most Daring Rescue Force* (Crown Publishing). 2000.

Chairman of the Joint Chiefs of Staff Instruction (CJCSI) 3270.01A, dated July 2004

Daniels, Stephen Brewster, *Rescue from the Skies: The Story of the Airborne Lifeboats* (Seven Hills Publishing). 1996.

DOD Directive 1300.7, *Training and Education Measures Necessary to Support the Code of Conduct.*

DOD Instruction 1300.21, *Code of Conduct Training and Education*

Falzone, Joseph J., *Combat Search and Rescue; CSEL Enhancements for Winning Air Campaigns* (Air University Press). 1997.

Franks, Norman L. R., *Another Kind of Courage: Stories of the UK-based Walrus Air-Sea Rescue Squadrons* (Sparkford Press). 1994.

Grant, W. T., *Wings of the Eagle: A Kinsmen's Story* (Ivy Books). 1994.

Guilmartin, John F., *A Very Short War: The* Mayaguez *and the Battle of Koh Tang* (College Station: Texas University Press). 1995.

Hansen, Wallace R., *Greenland's Icy Fury* (Texas A & M University Press). 1994.

Kelly, Mary Pat, *"Good to Go": The Rescue of Captain Scott O'Grady, USAF, from Bosnia* (Naval Institute Press). 1996.

Koskinas, Ioannis, *Black Hats and White Hats: the Effect of Organizational Culture and Institutional Identity on the 23rd Air Force* (Maxwell AFB: School of Advanced Air and Space Studies thesis). 2004.

McConnell, Malcolm, *Into the Mouth of the Cat: The Story of Lance Sijan, Hero of Vietnam* (Replica Publishing). 1997.

Risner, Robinson, *The Passing of the Night: My Seven Years as a Prisoner of the North Vietnamese* (Ballantine Books). 1992.

Ryan, Paul B., *The Iranian Rescue Mission: Why It Failed* (Naval Institute Press). 1985.

Taylor, L. B., *That Others May Live: The Aerospace Rescue and Recovery Service* (Dutton Press). 1967.

Tilford, Earl H., *Search and Rescue in Southeast Asia, 1961-1975* (Office of Air Force History). 1980.

Woodward, Bob, *Bush At War* (Simon and Shuster). 2003.

Veda Incorporated, *Combat Search and Rescue Report to the Joint Chiefs of Staff and the Executive Agent for Combat Search and Rescue: Combat Search and Rescue Requirements and Capabilities Study* (Veda Incorporated, Washington D.C.). 1997.

Veith, George J., Code *Name Brightlight: The Untold Story of US POW Rescue Efforts During the Vietnam War* (Free Press). 1998.

Whitcomb, Darrel D., *The Rescue of BAT 21* (Naval Institute Press). 1998.

GLOSSARY

Abbreviations and Acronyms

AAF	Army Air Force
ACC	Air Combat Command
AFDD	Air Force doctrine document
AFSB	afloat staging base
AFSOF	Air Force special operations forces
AFTTP	Air Force tactics, techniques, and procedures
AMC	airborne mission commander
ANG	Air National Guard
AOC	air and space operations center
ARRS	Aerospace Rescue and Recovery Service
ARS	Air Rescue Service
ATO	air tasking order
AWACS	airborne warning and control system
C2	command and control
C2ISR	command, control, intelligence, surveillance, and reconnaissance
CAF	combat air forces
COMAFFOR	commander, Air Force forces
COMJSOTF	commander, joint special operations task force
CRO	combat rescue officers
CSAR	combat search and rescue
CSARTF	combat search and rescue task force
DOD	Department of Defense
DODI	Department of Defense instruction
FAC	forward air controller
FAC(A)	forward air controller (airborne)
FE/FDO	force enhancement/flexible deterrent option
FOB	forward operating base
FOL	forward operating locations
IAW	in accordance with
IP	Isolated personnel
ISOPREP	isolated personnel report
ISR	intelligence, surveillance, and reconnaissance
JAOC	joint air operations center (JP 1-02); joint air and space operations center {USAF}
JFACC	joint force air component commander (JP 1-02); joint

	force air and space component commander {USAF}
JFC	joint force commander
JFSOCC	joint force special operations component commander
JP	joint publication
JPRC	joint personnel recovery center
JSOTF	joint special operations task force
JTF	joint task force
JTTP	joint tactics, techniques, and procedures
LO	low-observable
LOAC	laws of armed conflict
MAC	Military Airlift Command
MAJCOM	major command
MARLO	Marine liaison officer
MOB	main operating base
NALE	naval liaison element
OIF	Operation IRAQI FREEDOM
OEF	Operation ENDURING FREEDOM
OPCON	operational control
OPLAN	operation plan
OPORD	operation order
OPSEC	operations security
OSC	on-scene commander
PJ	pararescuemen (replaced pararescue jumper specialists)
PR	personnel recovery
PRCC	personnel recovery coordination cell
PRO	personnel recovery operations
PRDO	personnel recovery duty officer
PRPO	personnel recovery plans officer
RESCAP	rescue combat air patrol
RESCORT	rescue escort
RMC	rescue mission commander
ROE	rules of engagement
RT	recovery team
SAR	search and rescue
SEAD/DEAD	suppression/destruction of enemy air defenses
SecDef	Secretary of Defense
SERE	survival, evasion, resistance, escape
SOLE	special operations liaison element
SPINS	special instructions
STT	special tactic teams

TACON	tactical control
TPFDD	time-phased force and deployment data
TPFDL	time phased force deployment list
US	United States
USAF	United States Air Force
USJCOM	United States Joint Forces Command
USSOCOM	United States Special Operations Command
UTC	unit type code

Definitions

airborne mission coordinator. The coordinator who serves as an extension of the executing component's personnel recovery coordination cell (PRCC) and coordinates the recovery effort between the combat search and rescue task force (CSARTF) and the PRCC (or joint personnel recovery center) by monitoring the status of all CSARTF elements, requesting additional assets when needed, and ensuring the recovery and supporting forces arrive at their designated areas to accomplish the PR mission. The component PRCC or higher authority may designate the AMC. The AMC appoints, as necessary, an on-scene commander. Also called **AMC**. (AFDD 2-1.6)

combat search and rescue. Combat search and rescue is how the Air Force accomplishes the personnel recovery task. It is the Air Force's preferred mechanism for personnel recovery execution in uncertain or hostile environments and denied areas. Also called **CSAR**. (AFDD 2-1.6)

combat search and rescue mission coordinator. The designated person or organization selected to direct and coordinate support for a specific combat search and rescue mission. Also called **CSAR mission coordinator**. (JP 1-02)

evasion and escape. The procedures and operations whereby military personnel and other selected individuals are enabled to emerge from an enemy-held or hostile area to areas under friendly control. Also called **E&E**. (JP 1-02)

evasion and recovery. The full spectrum of coordinated actions carried out by evaders, recovery forces, and operational recovery planners to effect the successful return of personnel isolated in hostile territory to friendly control. (JP 1-02)

isolated personnel. Military or civilian personnel separated from their unit or organization in an environment requiring them to survive, evade, or escape while awaiting rescue or recovery. Also called **IP** (JP 1-02)

isolated personnel report. A Department of Defense Form (DD 1833) containing information designed to facilitate the identification and authentication of an evader by a recovery force. Also called **ISOPREP**. (JP 1-02)

joint force air component commander. The commander within a unified command, subordinate unified command, or joint task force responsible to the establishing commander for making recommendations on the proper employment of assigned, attached, and/or made available for tasking air forces; planning and coordinating air operations; or accomplishing such operational missions as may be assigned. The joint force air component commander is given the authority necessary to accomplish missions and tasks assigned by the establishing commander. Also called **JFACC**. See also joint force commander. (JP 1-02) *[The joint air and space component commander (JFACC) uses the joint air and space operations center to command and control the integrated air and space effort to meet the joint force commander's objectives. This title emphasizes the Air Force position that air power and space power together create effects that cannot be achieved through air or space power alone.]* (AFDD 2) {Words in brackets apply only to the Air Force and are offered for clarity.}

joint personnel recovery center. A primary joint personnel recovery (PR) node. The center is suitably staffed by supervisory personnel and equipped for planning, coordinating, and executing joint PR within the geographical area assigned to the joint force. The facility is operated jointly by personnel from two or more Service or functional components or it may have a multinational staff of personnel from two or more allied or coalition nations. Also called **JPRC.** (AFDD 2-1.6)

military deception. Actions executed to deliberately mislead adversary military decision makers as to friendly military capabilities, intentions, and operations, thereby causing the adversary to take specific actions (or inactions) that will contribute to the accomplishment of the friendly mission. The five categories of military deception are: a. strategic military deception—Military deception planned and executed by and in support of senior military commanders to result in adversary military policies and actions that support the originator's strategic military objectives, policies, and operations. b. operational military deception—Military deception planned and executed by and in support of operational-level commanders to result in adversary actions that are favorable to the originator's objectives and operations. Operational military deception is planned and conducted in a theater of war to support campaigns and major operations. c. tactical military deception—Military deception planned and executed by and in support of tactical commanders to result in adversary actions that are favorable to the originator's objectives and operations. Tactical military deception is planned and conducted to support battles and engagements. d. Service military deception—Military deception planned and executed by the Services that pertain to Service support to joint operations. Service military deception is designed to protect and enhance the combat capabilities of Service forces and systems. e. military deception in support of operations security (OPSEC)—Military deception planned and executed by and in support of all levels of command to support the prevention of the inadvertent compromise of sensitive or classified activities, capabilities, or intentions. Deceptive OPSEC measures are designed to distract foreign intelligence away from, or provide cover for, military operations and activities. (JP 1-02)

on-scene commander. The person designated to coordinate the personnel recovery efforts at the recovery site. Also called **OSC**. (AFDD 2-1.6)

operational control. Transferable command authority that may be exercised by commanders at any echelon at or below the level of combatant command. Operational control is inherent in combatant command (command authority). Operational control may be delegated and is the authority to perform those functions of command over subordinate forces involving organizing and employing commands and forces, assigning tasks, designating objectives, and giving authoritative direction necessary to accomplish the mission. Operational control includes authoritative direction over all aspects of military operations and joint training necessary to accomplish missions assigned to the command. Operational control should be exercised through the commanders of subordinate organizations. Normally this authority is exercised through subordinate joint force commanders and Service and/or functional component commanders. Operational control normally provides full authority to organize commands and forces and to employ those forces as the commander in operational control considers necessary to accomplish assigned missions. Operational control does not, in and of itself, include authoritative direction for logistics or matters of administration, discipline, internal organization, or unit training. Also called **OPCON**. (JP 1-02)

pararescue team. Specially trained personnel qualified to penetrate to the site of an incident by land or parachute, render medical aid, accomplish survival methods, and rescue survivors. (JP 1-02)

personnel recovery. The sum of military, diplomatic, and civil efforts to effect the recovery and return of US Military, DOD civilians, and DOD contractor personnel who are isolated or missing while participating in a US government-sanctioned military activity or missions in an uncertain or hostile environment, or as determined by the Secretary of Defense. Also called **PR**. (CJCSI 3270.01A and AFDD 2-1.6)

personnel recovery coordination cell. A primary personnel recovery facility suitably staffed by supervisory personnel and equipped for coordinating and controlling personnel recovery operations. The facility is operated unilaterally by personnel of a single Service or jointly by functional component. For Navy component operations, this facility may be called a rescue coordination team. Also called **PRCC** (or **RCT** for Navy component). (AFDD 2-1.6)

recovery teams. Designated Air Force teams specifically trained to operate independently or in conjunction with rotary wing / fixed wing aircraft, watercraft and overland vehicles. Combat rescue officers (CRO), pararescue specialists and survival, evasion, resistance, escape specialists, provide this capability. Also called **RT** (AFDD 2-1.6)

special tactics team. An Air Force team composed primarily of special operations combat control and pararescue personnel. The team supports joint special operations by selecting, surveying, and establishing assault zones; providing assault zone terminal guidance and air traffic control; conducting direct action missions; providing medical care and evacuation; and, coordinating, planning, and conducting air, ground, and naval fire support operations. Also called **STTs**. (JP 1-02)

tactical control. Command authority over assigned or attached forces or commands, or military capability or forces made available for tasking, that is limited to the detailed and, usually, local direction and control of movements or maneuvers necessary to accomplish missions or tasks assigned. Tactical control is inherent in operational control. Tactical control may be delegated to, and exercised at any level at or below the level of combatant command. Also called **TACON**. (JP 1-02)